POWERHOUSE EMAIL

How to Turn Strangers into Qualified Appointments with Email Marketing

Curtis W DeCora

POWERHOUSE EMAIL

Copyright © 2019 Curtis DeCora
All Rights Reserved.

ISBN-13: 9781704662244

Superior Marketing
9664 N County Road NN
Hayward, Wisconsin 54843
www.HaywardMarketing.us

Superior Marketing is a Native American owned Digital Marketing firm specializing in full spectrum Local Marketing and Sales Solutions. Superior Marketing is a dba and registered and licensed in the state of Wisconsin.

Printed in the United States
First Edition: November 2019

Book Design and Content by Curtis DeCora

POWERHOUSE EMAIL

POWERHOUSE EMAIL

ABOUT THE AUTHOR

Curtis DeCora is a Native American entrepreneur from the Lac Courte Oreilles Band of Lake Superior Chippewa in Hayward Wisconsin.

After 12 years of experience in the sales arena, Curtis has developed a wide range of strategies, techniques, tips and methods to produce results.

12 years includes experiences in numerous capacities in the business development channel. Starting off as a Sales Associate in door-to-door security sales, moving into the role of Sales Development Representative (SDR), Account Executive, Senior Account Executive, Senior Sales Consultant, Territory Manager, and eventually moving into the role of Director of Sales, and Vice President of Sales for numerous companies.

Today, companies hire Superior Marketing to develop their internal sales processes for more efficient and cost-effective sales solutions increasing monthly recurring revenue and new account generation.

In 2019, Curtis has served over 200 businesses in four countries, and trained 81 sales professionals throughout the world to become more efficient and productive sales people for their own business and employer.

POWERHOUSE EMAIL

POWERHOUSE EMAIL

WHAT OTHERS ARE SAYING ABOUT SUPERIOR MARKETING

"Best freaking business resource EVER! From merchant services to SEO ranking services, web services, to pep talks no one does it better than Mr. DeCora. I can't possibly recommend/refer his services enough. In less than 24 hours of tinkering with our ranking, we have received three new direct reservations, one of which is booking our entire resort! If you're looking to get ahead of the competition and save on fees, give Curtis a call!"

- Cassy Wilkozek, Principal at Musky Joes Resort

"Truly outside of their class. Curtis went out of his way to help me on multiple occasions. Worth every penny! I highly recommend his and his team to anyone looking to expand their company's client base."

- Gilbert Tirado, Forex Trader at iMarkets LIve, Inc

"Mr. Curtis gave me some excellent actionable advice. He opened my eyes to the possibilities of prospecting for clients online. Some of which I had no idea of. Thanks for the sales training."

- Nalin Singh, SEO Consultant

POWERHOUSE EMAIL

"Curtis is a genius when it comes to sales development. He has incredible knowledge and experience whenever I talk to him, he gives me extra every time. I am really happy with the results and will highly recommend him."

- Abu Huraira, Social Media Manager at DevBatch, Inc

"Curtis DeCora gave me actionable, relevant and extremely valuable ideals I could implement in the same day to improve my sales skills and increase prospects in my business. I am really excited to continue to work with him and see my business grow! Thank you!"

- Jennifer Lee, Technical Consultant

"Gotta give a shout out to the awesome DeCora. This guy is a beast in terms of sales. He knows everything. Also, I was amazed by his charisma and openness to help others. I received tons of great advice from Curtis and he was kind enough to provide me with tons of free tools regarding lead generation. 10/10"

- Vija Liviu Robert, CEO at Start Small Digital

"Superior Marketing is an excellent organization who can help you accomplish your goals. Next time you'd like to grow, they can help!"

POWERHOUSE EMAIL

- Nick Dash, Nutritional Consultant at MealCraft

"Curtis is a very knowledgeable and thorough man. He takes the time that's needed to understand what you need and finds the right tools to get the job done!"

- Darren Landgren, Principal at Landgren Fabrications

"Superior Marketing really helped me out with filling our sales pipeline to make sure our internal team had the leads to follow up and close. I will keep using them because they offer a great service and value which far exceeds their price."

- Marcel Bayon, CEO at Kawsah

"One of the best companies I have worked with in regards to sales, lead generation and marketing. Hit them up for any sales needs, they have something for everyone."

- Prerak Trivedi, Graphic Designer

"Superior Marketing has a solid ground game and excellent customer service. Our sales team has benefited immensely from their resources and tools."

- Aaron Carmody, CEO of Streamline Consulting

POWERHOUSE EMAIL

POWERHOUSE EMAIL

TABLE OF CONTENTS

INTRODUCTION	12
BUILDING A LIST	18
Cold Email Lists	19
Opt-In Email Lists	27
HOW TO CAPTURE EMAILS	32
10 Powerful Methods to Capture Emails	33
HOW TO MANAGE YOUR EMAIL LIST	47
CREATING A VALUE LADDER	56
STRANGERS TO QUALIFIED APPOINTMENTS	67
THE POWERHOUSE PLAYBOOK	81
CONCLUSION	90
THANK YOU	104

POWERHOUSE EMAIL

CHAPTER 1

INTRODUCTION

POWERHOUSE EMAIL

INTRODUCTION

Email marketing is the act of sending an electronic commercial message, typically to a group of people, using email. In its broadest sense, every email sent to a potential or current customer could be considered email marketing[1].

According to **OptIn Monster**, the definition of Email Marketing is:

> Email marketing is the highly effective digital marketing strategy of sending emails to prospects and customers. Effective marketing emails convert prospects into customers, and turn one-time buyers into loyal, raving fans.

Email is an extremely cost-effective component of your digital marketing strategy. The majority of businesses in operation today are not using email as part of their prospecting process.

Email Marketing can cost you pennies on the dollar in relation to new-aged methods, and generate upwards of 20 times more than your initial investment.

---

[1]Email Marketing: Wikipedia Definition

POWERHOUSE EMAIL

In some instances with clients I service, the majority of their revenues are produced from email marketing campaigns.

Let me explain. I'm a big believer of using MailChimp, it's a super simplistic email service provider with a drag-and-drop interface.

While Mailchimp is striving to become an all-in-one marketing platform, they're bread and butter is still the email marketing tools they offer.

Did you know the average open rate across all email marketing campaigns is 20.81%?

What does that mean?

That means that if you're running a campaign with 1,000 emails in your list, 208 emails will be opened.

Why is that significant?

The average organic reach on Facebook posts is 6.4%, according to Social Media Today. That means, if that same 1,000 users who opted in to your email list by way of your Facebook page, only 64 people will see your organic posts.

Comparatively speaking, email would provide a 325% greater reach than an organic Facebook post.

This is why social media posts require engagement.

POWERHOUSE EMAIL

While Facebook posts are free, they do require posts that encourage engagement; likes, comments, shares and tagging friends.

Example 1: Community Event Announcement

24	0	Boost Unavailable
People Reached	Engagements	
👍 Like	💬 Comment	↗ Share

In this Facebook page I took over, there is a page that had 343 page likes, only 24 people were reached with this post. There are 0 engagements, meaning it is highly unlikely that anyone will see the post without any prior engagement.

Example 1a: Facebook Page LIkes

 343 people like this

How to Get Engagement Plus Build Your Email List

So, in this example a standard post with zero engagement, the organic reach is in fact 6.99%, which isn't far from the average of 6.4%.

Let's say we run an engagement post, whereas the individuals who liked the page can enter a drawing for a free product. This could be a free 12-pack of soda for a

POWERHOUSE EMAIL

local convenience store, a free window cleaning, or any other free service. In addition to the opt-in you're asked to

1. Like
2. Comment "Free"
3. Share on your page

Each action taken

1. Entry
2. Like
3. Comment
4. Share

Each action gets an additional entry into the drawing. In this case, you would get 4 entries into the drawing for the free product or service.

These are 100% free options to get your 343 to see the post as well as those who see the post which they share.

In the past, I have done this with clients and a brand new Facebook page with less than 100 page likes would get a reach of 3,000+ simply by sharing the post and leveraging their friends and followers.

In short, you were able to get organic post engagement, generate new page likes, and build your email list all in one single post.

POWERHOUSE EMAIL

CHAPTER 2

BUILDING A LIST

BUILDING A LIST

The most critical part of running a successful email campaign is to build a list.

Let's look at a couple of ways to build a list.

Cold Email Lists

The most common email marketing in today's business environment is to spam cold email lists.

> **NOTE:** I DO NOT ADVOCATE FOR THIS METHOD

However, if you're interested in learning how people are leveraging the cold email marketing method, I'll be happy to share that strategy with you.

Here are two methods to obtain a bulk email list within your ideal client profile niche and blasting an entire list.

1. Buy a List

You work with a list provider to find and purchase a list of names and email addresses based on demographic and/or psychographic information. For example, you might purchase a list of 50,000 names and email addresses of people who live in Minnesota and don't have children. There are several sustainable ways to

POWERHOUSE EMAIL

use email marketing to grow your business. This isn't one of them.

Once you buy this list, you can simply export them into an email service provider like MailChimp, Constant Contact, Drip, SendinBlue, Convert Kit, AWeber, GetResponse, OptInMonster, ActiveCampaign, SendLane, iContact, MilkShake, SendGrid, and so on. These are all email marketing software platforms that allow you to send emails to bulk email addresses.

2. Rent a List

This is an option, whereas a "Digital Marketing Agency" will work with you to create an initial message, segmentation, niche and using their email marketing list they have built, will run the email campaigns for you.

You never get to see the emails, view the initial message, or responses leading to what the provider considers a "lead."

This is an option I'm seeing most new-age digital entrepreneurs are using to generate appointments, calls, or call-backs.

They may send an email with 10,000 email addresses and get you 10 responses. Those 10 responses are considered "leads" and they'll send you the name, and phone number of the prospect who responded.

POWERHOUSE EMAIL

Unfortunately, you don't know the message sent or which offer they're responding to. This is rolling the dice with your money and business reputation.

3. Build Your Own Cold Email List

In the past, I have done this, and still do this today but very minimally. I typically do this when I find a targeted list matching my Ideal Client Profile and use the cold email as a follow up to my initial first two steps.

My initial first two steps include:

    a. **Cold Call**: I call the prospect, leave a short, detailed message, with a big claim and offer to send some documentation. If they find it important and relevant, we can schedule a call to discuss. If this goes to voicemail, I'll leave said voicemail and move to Step B;

    b. **Social Media Message**: I'll leave an initial message referencing the voicemail and ask their permission to email them some documentation on a particular offer or opportunity.

THEN, and only then, do I mine for their email address.

These two simple tools and browser plugins allow for you to find email addresses for targeted prospects and help build your list to obtain contact information.

POWERHOUSE EMAIL

Hunter.io

Hunter.io is an online software-as-a-service (SaaS) tool that scrapes websites for contact information

Hunter.io is a very simple Google Chrome plugin that allows you to scrape websites for contact information.

This is about 60% successful as most of your larger prospects using an email address with their primary domain name. In other instances where they use a different domain name specifically for email usage, you will likely not find an email address.

Example 2: Hunter.io email scraping software

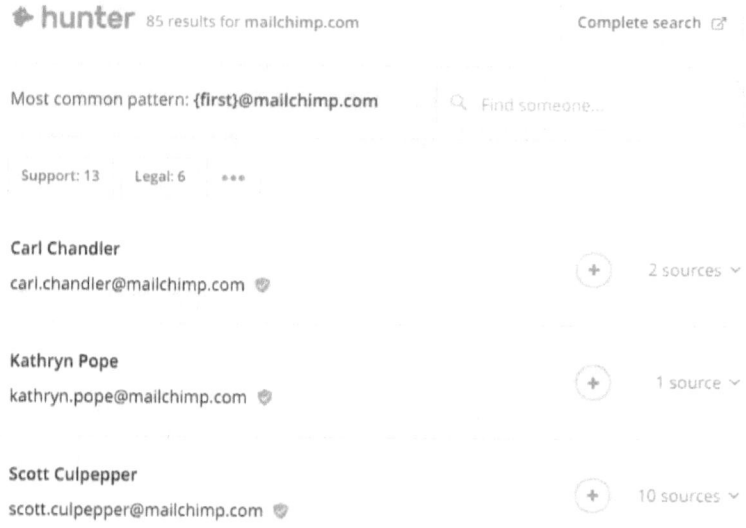

POWERHOUSE EMAIL

If I were prospecting MailChimp as a potential client and had something of value they could use to create additional opportunities for their business. I would use Hunter.io to pull email addresses.

Contact◉ut ContactOut

ContactOut is a recruitment sourcing tool used by 30% of Fortune 100 companies. Our users include Microsoft, MERC, and Bank of America. ContactOut adds a powerful overlay on top of LinkedIn profiles that displays phone numbers, email addresses, and social media profiles

Example 3: ContactOut of Grant Cardone

Contact◉ut ≡

✉ grantcardonelinkedin@gmail.co
✉ grant@grantcardone.com
📞 310-777-0255 (Work)
🐦 GrantCardone
🔍 Find work email »

⬇ Save Profile ▼
▦ View Saved Profiles
▤ Notes

This is a screenshot of Grant Cardone's information. Now, this is public domain and accessible to anyone, and on his website.

However, this is just an example of what ContactOut can do for you while mining for contact details.

POWERHOUSE EMAIL

Why you shouldn't tread lightly with cold email

1. Violating GDPR Rules of Consent

You are legally required to allow the recipient to opt-out of the email list, and if you're buying lists or renting lists, this isn't always followed and often neglected.

If you're prospect is operating and/or residing in Europe, they're protected under the May 2018 GDPR act.

What is the GDPR Act?

General Data Protection Regulation Act of 2018. Under this act you must obtain explicit consent from your prospects to send them email correspondence.

2. Reputable Email Service Providers Crackdown

If you're using a reputable email service provider, or email marketing software, you're deliverability will be pinged for sending emails to those who did not opt-in.

In MailChimp, there is a check box that asks, "Do you have permission to send emails to this address?"

If you check that box and any one of the recipients report your email as Spam, your account will be suspended and likely locked.

Your email can be scored and deemed as an entity that sends unsolicited spam.

POWERHOUSE EMAIL

3. Google Email Addresses Are Not For Sale

Let's think about this one for a minute. If that email address worked and was highly responsive, why would anyone sell that list?

If someone was generating new clients, increasing revenues, and producing exponential results, why would they turn around and sell that list?

The only instance where a responsive email list would be for sale, is if you were merging with another business, acquiring a new business customer list, or in some cases, doing joint venture marketing and their valued customers are aware of the joint venture effort.

Plain and simple. Do not buy or rent email lists.

4. They Don't Know Who You Are

In short, if you're buying or renting lists, you have to come to terms that the prospect has zero idea of who you are, or what your business does.

The new methodology, which needs to find a deep dark hole to go into and sleep for a very long time, is the cold email with the headline, "Question…" and hoping for a response.

Even if you get an open, but ask a question that provides zero value and you're simply trying to schedule an appointment with no prior experience with you, your company or your offer.

Yes, you can prospect, but tricking people into a phone appointment isn't going to end well.

Consider this, when was the last time a random doctor called you, and said, "Quick Question... If I could show you how to improve your health with just a 30 minute visit?"

Let's say you took the bait and showed up for the appointment.

In that appointment, they wanted to give you a rectal exam without any prior knowledge.

Would you be urged to pay for that rectal exam and any part of their upsale on their value ladder?

While that is an extreme example, it is very much similar with the new-aged cold email tactics and tricks.

5. You Harm Your Deliverability and IP Reputation

If you're an entrepreneur sending out unsolicited cold emails, you run the risk of harming your IP reputation and your email deliverability is harmed.

In most cases, even if your "warm up" an email address, you still run the risk of ruining your IP reputation and email deliverability score.

6. Your Email Service Provide Will Penalize You

Yes, email service providers like Google, Yahoo and Outlook will penalize you and shut down your account for violating their terms of service.

I am not proud to admit that I lost 12 gmail addresses in 2017 by hiring a team of cold emailers, even after "warming up" the email address.

The end result?

I sent out emails to a list of 50,000 email addresses and produced just 10 appointments, and lost 12 email addresses.

That is not something I am proud of.

My personal email address has been in operation for 18 years, and I use it to conduct business, send out emails to prospects, clients and referrals.

Opt-In Email Lists

Now, let's explore how to properly build email lists that produce higher open rates, higher click-through rates, and ultimately higher conversion rates for more qualified appointments.

You can do this ethically and without violating any rules.

POWERHOUSE EMAIL

1. Use Lead Magnets

Whether you're leveraging organic posts which provide a free guide to DIY SEO, Making Healthy Meals for Diabetic Males, How to Lose 10 lbs in 30 days for Women, or any other form of free PDF document your ideal audience can consume. Exchange the document for an email address.

In the digital marketing world, scores of entrepreneurs are trying to find creative ways to leverage the power of LinkedIn to generate qualified leads.

I created a free report entitled, "9 Steps to LinkedIn Prospecting for Qualified Leads."

I sent this link out to fellow entrepreneurs, they shared it on their page for their fellow entrepreneur friends to view. Their associates, clients, and partners downloaded the free PDF. I was then awarded with 300+ email addresses for individuals specifically interested in prospecting on LinkedIn.

2. Create Useful Experiences

This allowed for me to craft out a 21 Day LinkedIn Prospecting Challenge email sequence on how to prospect on LinkedIn with proper messaging sequences and turn strangers into qualified appointments.

POWERHOUSE EMAIL

Those individuals who were interested in prospecting on LinkedIn followed the 21 Day LinkedIn Prospecting Challenge,, and were asked to report back their results.

Those who reported back their results were entered into another list of prospects offered a discounted service of Managed LinkedIn Prospecting using my Virtual Assistants.

I trained a team of Virtual Assistants to follow this simple LinkedIn prospecting process, which produced an average of 13 qualified appointments per every 100 prospects. 13% conversion rate isn't great, but that's 13 strangers that turned into qualified appointments.

3. Promote Those Results via Your Email List

Those prospects that didn't report back results, or didn't take you up on your discounted offer, are now seeing results from those who did take you up on your offer.

The social proof is extremely powerful, and are also those who they may already know, or associate with in smaller entrepreneurial groups.

In this example, I obtained 300+ optin email addresses to my list. 18 took me up on my discounted offer (5.8% conversion rate), and the 290 emails on my list were sent the results in an email campaign.

Out of those 290, I converted another 17 at the full price

for the Managed LinkedIn Prospecting service.

4. Replay the Hits

Once I was able to compile results and social proof, I created a blog post and shared that with my network on social media, once again.

This created an entirely new batch of interested individuals to download the "9 Steps to LinkedIn Prospecting for Qualified Leads" free PDF.

The cycle repeats itself.

I was able to get more email opt-ins to obtain the free PDF, then run the same process for the 21 Day LinkedIn Prospecting Challenge.

Those same participants were asked to report back their results in exchange for a discounted offer for Managed Linkedin Prospecting services.

What is the 21 Day LinkedIn Prospecting Challenge?

The challenge was a simple automated email campaign set up in MailChimp that sent out one unique email every single day with tips and techniques as to which steps to take in order to follow the process.

These 21 days included optimizing your LinkedIn profile, creating quality content for those viewing your profile, a clickthrough link to capture leads for their unique offer,

POWERHOUSE EMAIL

and how to leverage InMail to send out message sequences to convert strangers into qualified appointments.

CHAPTER 3

HOW TO CAPTURE EMAILS

HOW TO CAPTURE EMAILS

In the previous chapter, we discussed the process of capturing email addresses by way of a Lead Magnet.

Lead magnets are not the only way to build an opt-in email list.

There are numerous ways to create a high quality opt-in email list.

Let's explore some options to build out a high-quality opt-in email list.

without further adieu, my 10 powerful methods to capture opt-in emails.

10 Powerful Methods to Capture Emails

1. Cold Calling
2. Direct Mail
3. Host an Event
4. Lead Magnets
5. Free Giveaways
6. SEO & Blogging
7. Social Media Engagement Posts
8. Loyalty Programs
9. POS e-Receipts
10. Shopping Carts

POWERHOUSE EMAIL

1. Cold Calling

If you're engaging in any form of telemarketing or cold calling, you're in a prime position to speak with an individual on a one-one-one level and ask specific questions pertaining to your offer and qualify for best-fit.

In that call, I like to ask the prospect, "Where can I send you some information, to help you make an informed decision prior to scheduling an appointment?"

The most common positive-response is, "Sure. You can email me some information at *****@their-email.com"

This is a permission-based strategy to obtain their contact information to send them emails relevant to the cold call.

Go right ahead and send them a pitch deck, a presentation, video, sales slick, or newsletter to help them conduct their research prior to them making the decision to schedule that appointment.

2. Direct Mail

In any direct mail campaign, or "Direct Response Campaign" you want to make sure you have a call-to-action directing them to your website to opt-in to a free offer, lead magnet, event registration, giveaway, etc.

In most cases, I send out a sales letter, typed up, with

POWERHOUSE EMAIL

information on an exclusive offer they can redeem on my website, ideally a private url or page that isn't visible in the navigation menu.

This allows you to track the effectiveness of your campaign and determine the response rates with accuracy, while still gaining credit for the website traffic.

Example: YourWebsite.com/30-Day-Promo

You can redirect that domain to a private landing page with an exclusive page, and still gain credit for the web traffic on your primary domain.

These are by far the most effective methods of leveraging direct mail to capture opt-in email addresses.

3. Host an Event

In most instances, as an entrepreneur, you're an expert in your field, and hold vast amounts of knowledge only you can share with a thirsty crowd.

This is where you, as the subject matter expert, can host an event and invite individuals that fit your Ideal Client Profile to this event to learn more about your expertise.

The most effective method I have found is that the prospect takes advantage of your direct contact, again, whether by way of cold calls, direct mail, or social media message, receive a special offer. This could be free or

POWERHOUSE EMAIL

discounted for taking action today.

They can take action today, by going to your website and registering with their name, phone and email address, along with an added bonus.

My favorite question to ask as an added bonus includes, "Which topic do you want to learn more about?" A drop down option will include a series of services which you offer and topics you can provide insights, statistics, free reports, case studies, or handouts.

This allows you to capture an opt-in email address as well as a general idea of how to structure your event, based on the responses of your registrants.

4. Lead Magnet

Yes, we covered this partially, but I want to make sure we can gain some clarity on how to develop our very own lead magnets to capture opt-in emails.

Let's cover 10 ideas for a strong lead magnet

1. **Guide or Report**: This can be a simple guide to a process, or steps required to accomplish X, or annual report. These work really well for those looking for specific instructions or data to help drive their decision making process.

POWERHOUSE EMAIL

2. **Cheat Sheet:** A lot of people like to find short cuts, or summaries of books, courses, training, or system. These are great for capturing emails in exchange for a summary of your findings.

3. **Checklist:** I like to use checklists. If you're in a service based industry, checklists are great. Consider the last time you moved, I would bet you sat down and planned out your move 'hoping' you didn't forget something. I have a moving client, and we use a lead magnet entitled, "The Ultimate Moving Checklist" which gets downloaded an average of 6 times each month. Those are top-of-funnel prospects that can be nurtured into having them hire you as their moving company.

4. **Toolkit:** Toolkits are great for Do-It-Yourselfers who like to find out industry or trade secrets and try to test specific processes on their own. Provide them with a branded toolkit in exchange for an email address. Your followup sequence should be specific to the download and offering a helping hand to best navigate that toolkit.

POWERHOUSE EMAIL

5. **Free Courses**: Free courses are great lead magnets. In 2018, I offered free access to my Potent Prospecting course in Udemy in exchange for an email address. The email address helped me drive my book sales via an email campaign. The free course access offered fundamental concepts further explained in my book, and those who accessed the free course were offered my book at a discounted price of $5.00, versus the current price of $12.00

6. **Free Trial**: If you have a Software-as-a-Service, Platform-as-a-Service, or Managed Service; in some instances you can offer a free trial in lieu of an email address. Over the course of 7, 14 or 21 days, you can send them an automated email sequence loaded with tips and tricks to help them be successful with the software to convert them into paying customers on a monthly subscription pricing model.

7. **Discount/Free Shipping**: In the case of e-commerce, the most common email capture strategy is using an option to capture an email address for 15% off your order, or free shipping, to name a few. This is simple enough and if you

need me to elaborate, feel free to use the contact information at the end of this book to reach out.

8. **Quizzes and Surveys:** I get email surveys constantly from the software companies I use to run my business. These surveys are offered in exchange to unlock some new features offered in the upsale package. I get to trial test those new features free of charge for up to 7 days in exchange for a survey. If you're running a survey campaign as part of a "Research Phase" of your new venture, you can utilize this to capture email addresses.

9. **Pricing**: I know for a fact that a lot of service-based web companies do not share their pricing on subscription services. You must contact sales in order to see the pricing. However, some of those companies are getting more and more creative with their sales funnels. The creative companies are offering you an opportunity to see pricing after you clicked through their 2nd and 3rd levels of the sales funnel, viewing a series of videos and requesting your email address to access pricing. This is a

POWERHOUSE EMAIL

great way to capture an email address, however, I would question the longevity of that recipient to remain on the email marketing list.

10. **Webinar:** There are hundreds upon thousands of entrepreneurs using webinars to promote their business, and they're automating this process. The most common email capture method is to run an advertisement on social media, and the call-to-action is to join the free webinar, and your registration to this webinar captures your name and email address. In return they send you the details of a WebinarJam link and automated session of viewing.

5. Giveaways

This is a great and absolutely free way to build an email list, and one of my all-time favorites.

This is an example of a giveaway on the Facebook page, requiring likes, comments and shares, along with entering on the website with name, email and phone.

6. SEO & Blogging

I know this is something that most non-technical entrepreneurs may struggle with, however, if you're blogging and focusing on SEO (on-page and off-page), then you're in a prime position to generate web leads based on a blog post.

The best method to leverage SEO & Blogging is to go to Google, and type in a question in regards to a service you provide. If you're a carpenter, you may want to Google the term, "How to keep a deck clean." You will see the top websites in Google showing results for "10 Tips for Keeping Your Wood Deck Looking New."

Google is rewarding that website for writing a "response post" in their blog. Every single day 5.6 billion searches are conducted on Google, and an estimated 70% of them are questions.

Questions are best answered with a "response post." Those response posts can be best served with blogging.

It is highly recommended to leverage SEO & Blogging to attract web traffic. At the end of your blog post, make sure you have a lead magnet. This lead magnet can be something like, "The do-it-yourself deck on a budget." In this example, you'll attract individuals who are looking

POWERHOUSE EMAIL

---

to build a deck on a budget. If you're savvy enough to reach out to them via email you may be able to schedule an opportunity for a free, no-cost quote to build their deck.

7. Social Media Posts

Leverage your business page and personal page to share a blog post, lead magnet, giveaway or registration to an event.

According to a study conducted by BrandWatch, on average, a Facebook user has 383 friends. If you're levering both personal and business pages, you can exponentially increase the reach you may have from that post.

This is just another way to drive traffic to a specific offer in exchange of an opt-in email.

8. Loyalty Programs

Recall the last time you were in your local mall. Every single store you entered and made a purchase, you were always asked for your email address to join their loyalty program.

This is another method of gaining an opt-in email address for purposes of sending promotions, special offers, and news in email marketing campaigns.

It's a great way to capturing information and reducing

POWERHOUSE EMAIL

your marketing costs to facilitate future purchases.

Instead of running postcard mailer campaigns, Facebook Ads, or mainstream media advertising which can cost thousands upon thousands of dollars, you can leverage a loyalty program, which includes offering discounts in lieu of an email address.

The discount is still much cheaper than running $10,000 monthly advertising campaigns, and you're producing sales when you offer a discount. This is a direct correlation between marketing messages to sales, to discounts. If you don't make any sales from the promotion, you don't offer any discount. Whereas $10,000 advertising campaigns will not make any guarantees of generating sales.

9. POS e-Receipts

In today's retail environment, Point-of-Sale software now comes with a multitude of tools and options to supercharge your customer's checkout experience.

Let's use the example of a standard checkout.

Customer brings you product, you scan the item and report back the price, including tax.

The customer pays with cash or card.

After the transaction, you simply ask the customer, "Would you like me to email you the receipt and save

POWERHOUSE EMAIL

10% off your next purchase?"

This works like gangbusters for quick-serve restaurants.

The quick-serve restaurant can email the receipt and on that auto-generated receipt is a QR code or coupon code to apply to the next purchase, which is tracked in the POS system.

You generate an opt-in email address and bring in the customer for another experience.

Jon Taffer states, "*If somebody goes to a restaurant for the first time and has a flawless experience, the statistical likelihood of them doing a second visit is about 40%.*"

Increase that likelihood with a 10% off coupon while capturing an opt-in email address.

10. Shopping Carts

This is more applicable in e-commerce. In my coffee business, Boozhoo Premium Coffee, I generate upwards of 80% of my sales from my website.

When a customer checks out, they enter their email address for obtaining a tracking number with the United States Postal Service.

That email address gets dumped directly into my MailChimp segmented list.

POWERHOUSE EMAIL

An automatically generated email goes out thanking them for purchasing and supporting Boozhoo Premium Coffee.

In that email I include some blog posts to help them learn more about premium coffee and why it is superior to gourmet coffee, flavored coffee or regular coffee. Other topics include recipes to use in lattes and mochas.

I'm in the development phase of creating a PDF download to make your own bulletproof coffee using low-budget items found at your local grocer.

The PDF includes recipes and drinks they can consume to boost their metabolism, recommended cups per day, and how to leverage caffeine for a more beneficial workout for fat loss.

POWERHOUSE EMAIL

CHAPTER 4

HOW TO MANAGE YOUR EMAIL LIST

POWERHOUSE EMAIL

HOW TO MANAGE YOUR EMAIL LIST

Now, we're going to discuss the best practices for managing your email list.

I want to cover six simple steps to take in order to keep your list high-quality and high-engagement.

1. Regular Text Works Best

If you're considering creating a newsletter style email campaign, read this before you make your decision.

In Gmail, there are three (4 if you do it wrong) inboxes where emails are delivered.

In gmail, you have the three main inboxes.

1. Primary: This is where emails go from familiar email addresses or email addresses you saved. In some cases, a warmed up email address and reputable IP, they will end up here even if unsolicited.
2. Social: This is where you'll get your email notifications from a social media page you're following and requesting email notifications. Let's say you are subscribed to a Facebook Group. You'll get email notifications from that group

POWERHOUSE EMAIL

when someone posts a new status.

3. Promotions: This is where 99.99% of email newsletters will end up simply based on the structure and email software used to send the campaign. The majority of newsletter style emails will end up in this inbox. It is not necessarily a bad thing, but you're not in the primary inbox.

This is an example of an email newsletter that ends up in the promotional inbox of gmail.

More and more email service providers are segmenting your emails based on how they arrive.

If it is an html email, like this, it will likely end up in the promo inbox.

POWERHOUSE EMAIL

2. Storytelling

I get emails quite often from some of the email lists I subscribe to.

One of my most read emails come from Darren Hardy. Darren Hardy offers a daily email called the "Darren Daily." It is a basic text email with some pointers on motivation, time management, productivity and all of these emails come in the form of a story.

The story is compelling, the copy is strong, and the end of the email comes with a link to a call-to-action.

Another email list I subscribe to is Funk Roberts Fitness. Funk Roberts writes a strong email in all text, and at the end of the story, includes a link to learn more about that particular topic within the story.

3. Incorporate Video

One of the most simplistic click-through options you can utilize is a video.

Write a strong email with a story, and call-to-action to view the video explaining in detail the offer you're explaining.

Take a screenshot of the email, embed that in the bottom of the email and hyperlink the screenshot image directly to the video on your website.

POWERHOUSE EMAIL

This is very important.

You want to link the screenshot directly to your website so you get credit for that traffic. Once on your site and viewing the video, you will also get credit for the view in YouTube.

This is much more beneficial to your web metrics and authority of your site to link directly to your website, specifically, the page which includes the video.

4. Replay the Hits

If you're using Google Analytics, you can determine which pages, which topics, and which content is most viewed.

Create an email telling a story about a blog post topic. The topic could be about any one of your areas of expertise. Tell a specific story about that topic, it should be a real experience, then direct the readers to your blog post to learn more.

One your blog post, you should have your lead magnet, offer, or next step in your sales process. Some will convert, some won't. You live another day to run another email campaign promotion.

5. Segmenting Lists

This is one of the most important topics.

POWERHOUSE EMAIL

Let's say you run a digital marketing agency and offer web design, photography and videography.

Let's use the example of lead magnet opt ins.

Lead Magnet 1: 10 Web Design Tips for More Traffic

In this list, individuals want to learn more about tips and techniques to generate more traffic. A free PDF cheat sheet can be downloaded to access these 10 tips.

Lead Magnet 2: Top 3 cameras for DIY photography

In this list, individuals want to learn more about cameras, so they can do their own photography via a hobby. This may include a PDF download reviewing the top 3 cameras on the market, or the top three under $500.

Lead Magnet 3: Top 5 free video editing software

In this list, a how-to-guide to access these top 5 free video editing software and which features are offered with each software. The downloading of this PDF can help individuals learn how to edit videos with free software.

Where segmentation comes in handy and becomes extremely useful, is when you mismanage your email lists.

Let's say you wanted to run a $300 website promotion.

POWERHOUSE EMAIL

The wrong way to run this promotion is to combine all three lists and send out this promotion.

Here is why.

List 2 and List 3 did not opt in to be sold a website promotion. Some may have, but you'll find that you're going to see your list shrink due to recipients unsubscribing.

Your turned your informational list into a list you want to sell to.

Again, some may, but you're mismanaging your email list by doing this.

This is the number one cause of individuals unsubscribing from your email lists - mismanagement.

The most popular email marketing software options on the market allow you to segment your email lists and create campaigns specifically for that list.

Don't mismanage your email lists and segment properly.

6. Scrubbing and Engaging

Keep a close eye on your email list. Your reporting functions in your email software allow you to determine who is the most engaged, who opens your emails the most, who clicks through emails, and those who do not.

POWERHOUSE EMAIL

You will have some recipients on your email list that never open your emails.

It is very important to scrub your email lists free and clear of those not engaging.

Your email open rates will increase.

The significance of this -- you increase your email deliverability score and increase the reputation of your IP address.

If you're getting an email list that opens your emails consistently with an average open rate of 50% - that's a great open rate and 250% greater than the average email open rates, across all industries.

This was completed by scrubbing your list and managing your lists properly. As stated in the previous tip, segmenting your lists can also be a contributing factor in increasing your open rates, and increasing the deliverability score and reputation of your IP address.

POWERHOUSE EMAIL

POWERHOUSE EMAIL

CHAPTER 5

CREATING A VALUE LADDER

POWERHOUSE EMAIL

CREATING A VALUE LADDER

What is a value ladder?

A value ladder is a method of mapping out your product/service offering visually in ascending order of value and price. The value ladder allows you to cater to your client's needs no matter where they are at.

The value ladder isn't just a visual mapping of your offers, this is also the structure you want to follow in terms of moving your prospects along your sales cycles and converting them into paying customers.

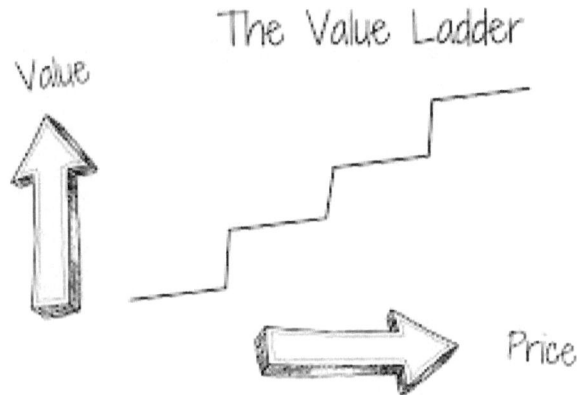

This is a value ladder.

As with any ladder, you start at the bottom, and ascend upwards to the top, which can include converting prospects to paying customers, and upsales.

POWERHOUSE EMAIL

The value ladder is similar to that of a sales funnel.

Every sales funnel starts with awareness. So, how we do we create awareness?

Lead magnets.

How do we generate interest?

Well, the Value Ladder!

Let's look at an example of a value ladder

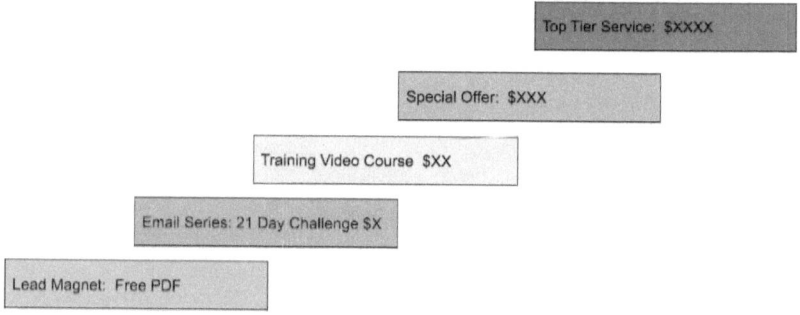

1. Lead Magnet

In this example we start with a lead magnet.

The lead magnet is 100% free of charge in exchange for an email address.

Once they download the free PDF, you can create an automated sequences with an email to join the 21 day challenge for $7.00.

POWERHOUSE EMAIL

2. Low-Level Offer

Once your prospects join the $7.00 21 Day Challenge, you're building trust, developing a relationship and giving tremendous amounts of value to your prospects for just $7.00.

Upon completion of the 21 Day Challenge email series, your 21st email can provide them with final instructions along with a special offer to join the video training course.

3. Mid-Level Offer

Once your low-level offer clients complete the 21 Day Challenge, either they completed the challenge specifically as outlined and achieved great success, and are eager for more.

This is where your mid-level offer comes into play.

Now, you can upsell them on your 21st email into a Video Training Course for $97.

Your video training course can come complete with access to your course software, access to a free Facebook Group with all of the current students, where they can chat and discuss any questions they may have. An additional benefit of the group is that you can answer any questions they may have in regards to the course details.

POWERHOUSE EMAIL

Upon completion of the Video Training Course, most course software offers a certificate of completion.

Any course software can send you a notification when someone completes your course.

4. High-Level Offer

Based on the results of the student having completed your course, you can move them further up the value ladder into a special offer.

"As a student having completed the Video Training Course, you're eligible for a special offer to access our Done-for-You System."

The special offer is Done-for-You System custom built for your business, your ideal client profile, and all content is developed with you.

This system is $999 one time payment, or 3 payments of $333.

The Done-for-You System is available to the general public at $3,000.

The student can elect to choose the Done-for-You System for a 66.67% discount as a reward for moving through your value ladder and dramatically reducing your marketing expenses.

The traditional marketing expenses required to

POWERHOUSE EMAIL

generate leads for high-level offer clients are 3x that of the offer. That's a general metric shared by Social Media Today.

The special high-level offer comes at a discount based on the previous revenues produced from:

- + $0 Lead Magnet
- + $7 Email Series
- + $97 Video Training Course

That's $104 in revenues coming from a free lead magnet.

If you generated this lead from a free social media post and captured an email address from an opt-in page, then you spent $0.00 and produced $104.

This is where the value ladder produces the greatest returns.

The student can choose the Done-for-You System...

or

5. Top-Tier Offer

If the student wishes to your agency do all of the work, and they'll simply conduct the fulfillment, you can offer the Top-Tier High-Ticket option of Managed Services for $1,500 per month on a 12 month agreement. This is a common option for entrepreneurs.

POWERHOUSE EMAIL

This option includes leveraging your team to build the system, manage the system, and send them converted clients and paying customers.

In this option, you would build out the entire system:

- Capture Page
- Lead Magnets
- Value Ladder
- Sales Funnel
- Website Content
- Social Media Page Management
- SEO
- Email Automation
- Email Series
- Video Training Course

When leads come through their system, your team would conduct the discover calls, qualified appointments, and assist with sales finalization.

This would be an example of a Top-Tier Offer.

The Benefits of a Value Ladder

The primary benefits of a value ladder include building trust by displaying authority, developing a relationship, and delivering high levels of value through content.

The content and value ladder do help the prospect understand the primary benefits of your services,

POWERHOUSE EMAIL

systems, processes, and how it can benefit their business.

The end results can come down to two options, like I showed in the example above.

You can move them through your lead magnet, right into an email series. The email series gives them a taste of what will be in the Video Training Course.

The Video Training Course shows them the full power of the system, services and processes.

Lastly, you move your student into a position to become a paying client.

As a paying client, they can choose to work the system themselves and hire a team to conduct the fulfillment and ongoing management.

Secondarily, they can hire your team to build and manage the entire system.

Traditional Sales Funnels vs the Value Ladder

In a traditional sales funnel, you would view an ad. The ad, once clicked, would take you to a sales page.

The sales page includes a video of features, advantages and benefits, along with social proof.

The social proof usually comes in the form of video testimonials, screenshots of reviews or comments, as

POWERHOUSE EMAIL

well as results.

The final step is a "Buy Now" button

The challenge which occurs... shopping cart abandonment.

<u>This is a volume game.</u>

You're sending thousands of individuals to your sales page and hoping for conversions. You pay to play in this game. You hope your video sales letter is strong enough to convert visitors into leads, leads into prospects, and prospects into paying customers.

There are numerous touchpoints from visitor to paying customer and a single sales letter will not suffice for higher conversion rates.

<u>Insert the value ladder.</u>

A value ladder walks visitors into a lead. The visitor becomes a lead by downloading your lead magnet.

The lead magnet becomes a prospect by engaging in your email series. A $7 investment does not guarantee the prospect automatically jumps into a $1,500 per month service.

The prospect now becomes a paying client by consuming your Video Training Series for $97, they learn your most valuable secrets as it relates to your

POWERHOUSE EMAIL

expertise.

As a consumer and student of yours, you're now in a position to ethically offer them an opportunity to build a business.

This business can be a Done-for-You System at $999 or Managed Service for $1,500 per month.

This is the biggest difference in a value ladder.

You're walking a prospect through your sales cycle in incremental stages, while building trust, establishing authority, and developing a relationship.

People from people they...

- + Know
- + Like
- + Trust

A video sales letter cannot build that for you, unless you establish a long-term remarketing campaign and send them drip email campaigns and hope they convert without low-level investments - or any investments for that matter.

POWERHOUSE EMAIL

ёPOWERHOUSE EMAIL

CHAPTER 6

STRANGERS TO QUALIFIED APPOINTMENTS

STRANGERS TO QUALIFIED APPOINTMENTS

Now that we know how to build a list, we know how to capture emails, and learned about properly managing email lists, and creating the value ladder....

We're going to show you how to turn strangers into qualified appointments.

What is a qualified appointment?

A prospect is a potential client who resembles the sellers ideal client profile but has not yet expressed interest in their products or services.

That's simple enough.

Additional considerations include:

+ Have an Immediate Need
+ Have Purchasing Power
+ Decision Making Authority

Personally, I would ensure the prospect matches the Ideal Client Profile, and has an immediate need to solve a problem or challenge, currently paying another vendor for lackluster results, as well as possesses the decision making authority for their organization.

Now, that we have identified what a qualified

appointment would look like, let's find out how to obtain qualified appointments.

Step 1: Lead Magnet

In your Lead Magnet you want to make sure you have something of massive value to prospects that match your Ideal Client Profile.

Leverage web builder software, and you can choose from:

- + LeadPages
- + InstaPage
- + BuilderAll
- + Karta
- + PhoneSites
- + ClickFunnels
- + MailChimp Landing Pages

POWERHOUSE EMAIL

You can utilize literally any landing page builder to capture emails in exchange for downloading your free lead magnet.

There are two ways you can launch this campaign.

The Lead Magnet can contain a link to the 21 Day Challenge on the last page of the PDF.

That PDF takes them directly to the registration page for the 21 Day Challenge.

There is a registration link and a checkout page. The low-level offer.

Now, you want to go to your email list. Take your email list and create a campaign.

Email	First Name	Last Name	City	Date of Birth
henry.l@hotmail.com	Henry	Lawson	Albuquerque	06/28/1973
marie.murray@gmail.com	Marie	Murray	San Fransisco	02/12/1991
jackprc@gmail.com	Jack	Price	New-York	09/05/1979
pstuart@yahoo.com	Paul	Stuart	Chicago	12/30/1986
emily.stevens@hotmail.com	Emily	Stevens	Denver	01/24/1982
kate-lee@gmail.com	Kate	Lee	Seattle	05/12/1996

Step 2. Create Email Campaign

This is an example of a landing page to promote your low-level offer.

POWERHOUSE EMAIL

Example: the 21 Day Challenge.

The email campaign would begin with mainly text, and begin telling a story about something related to your 21 Day Challenge.

At the end of the email, you insert a link directly to the 21 Day Challenge.

The link would arrive at a landing page like the one shown above.

In this example, it is wise to utilize a low-level offer. In most cases, a common low-level offer would include a $7 price tag. This is a simple low-level investment for anyone interested in learning more about your products, services or solutions.

Throughout the 21 Day Challenge, they'll learn specific tips, techniques, and steps as it relates to your intended methodology.

POWERHOUSE EMAIL

Step 3: Schedule Personal Contact

Near the end of your 21 Day Challenge, make sure you incorporate some opportunities to schedule a personal contact. I am extremely vague with the term, "Personal Contact" because every business does have a very different type of personal contact for you to deliver the most value.

Here are some examples of personal contact you can leverage:

- + Google Hangout
- + Discover Call
- + Live Webinar
- + Skype
- + On-Site Appointment
- + Group Presentation (geo specific)

Just to name a few, you can get an idea of what I mean by personal contact. In this step, you want to ensure that you're allowing your current low-level clients to ask

POWERHOUSE EMAIL

questions, explore a free topic discussion, or promote your mid-level offer, and share some data and case studies from your high-level clients or top-tier clients.

Step 4: Free Trial

If you're in account-based sales and marketing, this is something you can leverage as a means to collect data and get prospects that meet your ideal client profile into your sales pipeline.

If you're in SaaS, course sales, mentoring services, online training, or any other form of recurring revenue model sales, this is for you.

I'm sure you're already engaging in this type of acquisition strategy. The majority of companies offer a free trial, and allow your prospects to add their information, upload their account details, and perhaps upload their company data. This is your opportunity to let them touch, feel, and experience your offering. This

POWERHOUSE EMAIL

is an experiential strategy. Consider the mattress industry. The majority of mattress companies are now offering a 100 nights free. LinkedIn even has a free trial to test LinkedIn.

The primary benefit of this strategy is, again, experiential. You want your prospects to commit to your platform. Once they're committed, I personally feel that most companies miss the mark with follow up and onboarding. I am involved in dozens of entrepreneurial groups, and PhoneSites in the latest craze in these groups. I have tried the PhoneSites software for 14 days. During those 14 days, I had some questions. I created a few landing pages or sales pages, to opt in, and just couldn't see the total value of the price tag, whereas MailChimp offered the same exact form of landing page.

Here is the difference between one platform, from the other. MailChimp has an automated sequences. Once you opt-in to the paid version of MailChimp to create landing pages. You get marketing emails immediately with, "How to get started with landing pages." Another one included, "The top converting landing pages", and "How to segment data from your landing pages." All of this was extremely helpful for a new user.

PhoneSites, they really didn't have a follow up sequence to help with best practices and some initial steps you can take to make the most of your free trial.

Step 5: Convert to a High-Level Offer

Let's take this a step further into the next steps after the 14 day, 21 day or 30 day free trial.

This is the most common form of high-level offer in today's business environment.

There are a lot of companies that dive into, "Done for You" solutions.

Let's say you're taking your software, training platform, online courses, or equipment offer to the next level.

A "Done for You" services can go a long ways into converting your prospective clients into paying customers.

Let's use the example of Management Training.

In Management Training platforms, you can download

POWERHOUSE EMAIL

the ebook and learn the trade secrets of some of the most prominent management consultants around the world. Secondly, engaging in the 21 Day Challenge allows you to test some of those trade secrets, tips and techniques. If those are fruitful, then you can engage in a Personal Contact and ask any questions you might have in regards to the ebook and 21 Day Challenge. In this call, you get to drill down on specifics as it relates to your business. In this free Personal Contact opportunity, you're likely upsold into a free trial.

The most common script I hear on those free webinars includes, "As a reward for coming this far with our free information, I want to extend to you a free trial."

You're moving up the value ladder, and you're able to do this with your prospective clients, as well. The saying goes, "If it isn't broke, don't fix it." I would say that is true, to a certain extent.

Now, the free trial expires and it is time to get off the pot and make a decision.

If you find great value is the content thus far, you're likely in a position to utilize a "Done for You" service, whereas the vendor builds out your entire structure; whether it is management training, online courses, sales funnels, marketing automation, Software-as-a-Service, or any other "Done for You" service that would take time, energy and resources to build before you can

POWERHOUSE EMAIL

even consider seeing a quicker return-on-investment.

Vendor A may build out your entire structure so you can simply run your business with the right people, using the guidelines, templates and structure built for you.

This is your High-Level offer.

Step 6: Convert to a Top-Tier Offer

In most cases of management training, sales training, courses, software-as-a-service, or any other form of a recurring revenue model, this option exists with those who can not only teach, but can also deliver on their

POWERHOUSE EMAIL

very own strategies.

In 2017, when I was doing Managed LinkedIn Prospecting, I would walk all of the prospects through this same exact value ladder, and at the end of the free trial, I would offer two options:

a. **"Done for You" Service**: whereas the LinkedIn Prospecting process was completely done for the prospect. This would include optimizing their profile, developing downloadable assets, and creating a script for prospects to utilize while doing outbound InMail.
b. **Managed LinkedIn Prospecting**: This was a service I built out using Virtual Assistants. VAs would gain access to a clients' LinkedIn account and perform the prospecting, messaging, and targeting while managing responses and scheduling appointments.

In most cases, the clients would opt-in to the Managed Service. They simply wanted the appointment, not the structure or scripts.

The old adage states, "Sell the hole, not the drill."

This would ring true in this example.

While Superior Marketing performed a Managed LinkedIn Prospecting service, we would place clients on a monthly recurring payment plan. The Managed

POWERHOUSE EMAIL

Service would produce the hole, in this case, qualified appointments. We would pre-qualify through LinkedIn InMail, and if they met our client's qualification standards and Ideal Client Profile, we would have them book on our client's calendar.

The client would then participate on the call, and either convert the prospect or send them back to us for email nurturing and LinkedIn InMail follow up.

POWERHOUSE EMAIL

CHAPTER 7

THE POWERHOUSE PLAYBOOK

THE POWERHOUSE PLAYBOOK

I'm going to give you a simple playbook to follow to help you build your very own Powerhouse Email Strategy.

1. **Create Free Content**

    In this step we're talking about creating something of value that most of your prospects and paying customers are commonly asking for, or challenges to help facilitate buying decisions.

    This can be a free PDF, a Toolkit, a Free Guide, a Video Series, or something you can leverage in exchange of an email address.

    Again, this whole process is about building an email list.

2. **Create a Low-Level Offer**

    In this step, we want to create something that is extremely low-level, low-investment whereas they can test your strategies to determine if you're something to consider a trusted advisor.

    In the past, I had a 21 Day Prospecting Challenge. I called it, "The Daily 100s" and it was a 21 day gameplan to develop prospecting activities to help fill their pipeline.

    This Low-Level Offer was so effective, I now sell it

POWERHOUSE EMAIL

as a training program, but for 90 days.

However, prior to learning how effective it was for other sales professionals who were lacking sales training from their organization and wanted to gain a competitive advantage within their sales team.

The Daily 100s was sold for $21, and the message was, "$1 a day to a full sales pipeline." You can do the same and create some form of a low-level offer which brings more strangers into your pipeline via a low-level, low-investment offer.

3. **Make Personal Contact**

This is an extremely crucial step. I find it very important to create an opportunity for your low-level customers to engage in a personal contact opportunity.

This enables individuals or groups to ask questions about your first two offers. Typically, you'll find a lot of buying questions, "Will this work for Car Dealerships, Furniture Companies, Fireworks, MLM, etc"?

Those asking buying questions and raising buying signals are great prospects for your mid-level offer, while some are ready for the

POWERHOUSE EMAIL

high-level offer or top-tier offer.

Please gauge this with some identification of buying signals and prequalification.

Some of the top (free) tools you can use to create personal contact include: Google Hangouts, Skype, Facebook Live, YouTube Live, Blackboard Collaborate or Live Stream.

Leverage your email list to invite those to be present on this session and ask any questions they may have LIVE, and please be complete in your answers to ensure that you're delivering as much value as possible and maintaining your posture as the trusted advisor.

4. **Free Trials (When Possible) into Mid-Level Offer**

    This is the most common in Software-as-a-Service, Platform-as-a-Service, Equipment, Materials, or services.

    If you have the ability to offer a free trial, it is recommended to offer a free trial.

    Don't get me wrong, this isn't about giving in to the prospect and having them convert for $0.

    This is about gaining another level of commitment from the prospect and moving

POWERHOUSE EMAIL

them up your value ladder to the next position.

Each level of commitment gets you closer to a high-level customer or top-tier customer while also collecting revenue.

Some of the residual benefits of a free trial, while following this formula include; developing trust, building rapport, establishing a relationship and the continuation of the trusted advisor.

Take Note----- Please create an email series for those free trial prospects to help them navigate your free offer.

In some cases, this includes set up, navigation, usage, launching your first campaign, entering data, integrations, etc.

This goes a very long way - see the example of MailChimp vs PhoneSites.

In 2001, I ran across a gentleman by the name of Clate Mask, and he had this software called, "InfusionSoft."

Clate Mask had a twice-a-day email campaign that was automated with his software. This campaign was split into two emails.

Email #1 was how to set up your CRM. Email #2 was an example of a successful business using

POWERHOUSE EMAIL

InfusionSoft.

This continued for the 14 Day Free Trial. After setting up my account, importing data, and launching my first campaign.

I converted 2 paying clients within that 14 Day Free Trial. At this point in time, InfusionSoft was just $47 per month. It is now $199/mo and much more robust.

This was a great example of leveraging a Free Trial to convert a stranger into a paying customer.

5. **Create a High-Level Offer**

   Not everyone is going to have a "Done for You" service. In some cases, you can leverage your value ladder to move prospects into a high-level offer.

   After all, they have already gone through all of your free content, low-level offer, Personal Contact and mid-level offer.

   Perhaps the upsale into a high-level offer includes weekly calls, weekly audits, weekly training, or monthly reviews, etc.

   In your business, I'm more than confident you can come up with a high-level offer to convert strangers into high-level customers.

In most cases, a high-level offer includes a monthly recurring revenue model, this can be $599/mo, $999/mo or $1999/mo depending on your product, service or solution making it a reasonable offer in relation to others in your space requiring an upfront annual fee.

Let's use the example of software. There are still legacy software companies out there offering an annual software license.

If you're able to offer a monthly payments with the same level of support, and help companies manage their cash flow with monthly payments, you're more likely to win that business.

In the world of monthly options, these companies are taking the marketshare simply because it offers the same features, functionality, benefits and advantages without the full, up-front, investment.

6. **Create a Top-Tier Offer**

Let's be honest, we all want to have top-tier customers paying a premium and using our businesses' products, services or solutions to meet their challenges and needs.

POWERHOUSE EMAIL

How do we get to this point?

If we walk our prospects through the buyer's journey with a value ladder, we're more likely to convert strangers into top-tier customers.

All of my Top-Tier Sales Training clients came directly from the free PDF, moved into the 21 Day Challenge which I coined The Daily 100s, and opted in to the free Google Hangout session whereas I helped them develop their sales strategy, prequalification process, and process to sales finalization.

They moved into a $129 course on Udemy. After the Udemy course, I offered a $999 offer to build out their internal sales process, and most opted in to the $3,000 Outsourced Sales Solutions.

This included 4 Virtual Assistants doing all of the prospecting through email, social media, telemarketing, sales letters, ringless voicemails, sms texts, and joint venture marketing.

There you have it. The Powerhouse Playbook to leverage email for converting strangers to qualified appointments.

POWERHOUSE EMAIL

CHAPTER 8

CONCLUSION

CONCLUSION

In the previous chapter, you're seeing how a 6 Step Process can turn complete strangers into qualified appointments.

There are thousands of gurus in the marketplace today selling "Ads and Funnels."

The primary challenge with funnels includes, "Cart Abandonment."

What is Cart Abandonment

"Cart Abandonment is an ecommerce term used to describe a visitor on a web page who leaves that page before completing the desired action.

"Examples of abandonment include shopping cart abandonment, referring to visitors who add items to their online shopping cart, but exit without completing the purchase."

In the world of marketing automation and sales automation, there are a lot of sales pages visited, information filled out and transactions getting abandoned.

There are various reasons for cart abandonment, and I want to highlight some of those for you, here.

Top Reasons for Cart Abandonment

+ 34% were 'just looking' i.e. not ready to buy.
+ 23% had an issue with shipping.
+ 18% wanted to compare prices.
+ 15% decided to buy in-store instead.
+ 6% abandoned due to a lack of payment options.
+ 4% experienced a technical issue.

According to HubSpot, the average cart abandonment rate is 79.17%.

If you send 100 prospects to your sales page via marketing automation and sales automation, only 20 will convert.

What do you do with the other 80?

I would hope you nurture them in an email sequence and further the nurturing cycle.

Potential Revenue

What is potential revenue?

Potential revenue is a term brought about from the emergence of marketing automation and sales automation.

Potential revenue, in this case, is the term used to describe those 80 prospects that did not convert.

If each sale converted through your sales funnel by way

POWERHOUSE EMAIL

of marketing automation and sales automation were worth $997.

The conversion of 20 sales brought out $19,940 in revenue. However, the Potential Revenue includes $79,760.

What has been the most common strategy to solve this potential revenue challenge?

Humanizing the sales process! Insert the human.

I know it isn't as sexy as marketing automation and sales automation, but we're talking about $79,760 in revenue potential leaving the sales pipeline.

Cart Abandonment should include an immediate call from a Business Development Rep (BDR), or Sales Development Rep (SDR).

This call can be simple, non-invasive and address some of the questions the prospect may have.

The Difference between a Value Ladder and a Sales Funnel

The biggest difference between a value ladder and a sales funnel is **commitment**.

In a value ladder business development model, there are incremental increases in commitment from a free offer, low-level offer, mid-level offer, and ability to score your prospects prior to making an offer to a high-level offer or top-tier offer.

Let's take the example of a $997 offer.

The prospect may not fully know, like, and/or trust you as a business.

There may be additional concerns or priorities. In those instances, you likely need to identify some of those challenges.

In the case of cart abandonment, you're asking the prospect to know, like and trust you based on a sales letter, video sales letter, or sales page.

That's a tough nut to crack if you're not loading search engine ranking pages with massive amounts of content, videos, articles and social proof.

In the case of a value ladder, the prospect is getting to know who you are through your content, your strategies, tips and techniques and positioning yourself as the expert and advisor.

<u>Let me drill this one home.</u>

The top reason for cart abandonment is "not ready to buy." This should be an indication that you haven't yet addressed their primary issues, concerns, or delivered enough value in most cases.

POWERHOUSE EMAIL

A value ladder continually provides them with value. Value is delivered through your PDF download, your email challenge, free Persona Contact, and a free trial.

This includes four (4) levels of commitment.

The major comparison, here, is that a prospect has committed to your process four different times, whereas a sales funnel fully relies on the prospect's readiness.

In Powerhouse Email, you can continually nurture, prospect, present offers and deliver value through email and build a long-term client, versus hoping for a one-off sale with an 80% abandonment rate on your sales page.

Why do I advocate for email?

Let's look at a metric published by Social Media Today. Just 6.4% of all page likes and followers are seeing your organic posts.

While it is free to post on your business page, your page is only showing to an average of 6.4% of your likes and followers.

You can "Pay to Play" and boost your post, or run ads to get people to your website.

This is a push for engagement. If you're posting for engagement; likes, comments, tagging others and

POWERHOUSE EMAIL

sharing, then you're more likely to increase that metric.

According to an email benchmark study from MailChimp, according to user data from MailChimp software.

The average open rate across all verticals, industries and niches equals just 24.81%.

Comparatively speaking, **email marketing is 387% more effective** than organic posts from Facebook business pages.

Another major benefit of leveraging email marketing, you own your email list. If you're sourcing your email data from opt-ins, then you truly own that list.

In Facebook, you do not own your likes or followers, Facebook can regulate how many posts are viewed, and how many likes or followers are reached with your posts.

If we're looking at just open rates, we're missing the point of this book. SMS text messages and chatbots do have much higher open rates of 95%+, but the click-through rates are extremely low and most are violating CAN-SPAM or GDPR regulations.

According to research by the DMA (Direct Marketing Association) in 2018, for every $1 you spend on email marketing, you can expect $32 in return.

POWERHOUSE EMAIL

This is the highest return on investment above all the other marketing strategies.

Compare this with the Facebook Ads ROI of $2 for every $1 spent.

Email is a great tool to generate traffic to your website. Facebook can be a great platform allowing you to run specific ads to generate click-throughs to your landing page or website.

In most cases you can spend less than $1 to get a click, however, the true measure of effectiveness is conversion rates.

The conversion rates come by way of the landing page, sales page, squeeze page, or opt-in page.

If you're not converting initial visitors, you have to spend additional dollars to retarget them with new ads. Note, I mentioned you have to spend additional dollars.

In email marketing, you're simply nurturing them long-term and inserting prospecting customers into the value ladder at any point in time with your specific offers; free offer, low-level offer, direct contact, and/or mid-level offer.

It is recommended to have a prospect enter the value ladder on any one of the aforementioned levels prior to reaching your high-level offer or top-tier offer.

POWERHOUSE EMAIL

This is the optimal strategy to ensure you're doing the following:

+ Building Trust
+ Developing Rapport
+ Establishing a Position as Trusted Advisor
+ Delivering Value

Recommended Email Content Strategy

This is an important factor in determining your open rates, click-through rates and ultimately your conversion rates.

Do NOT Pitch and Persuade

The most common form of an email is to be vague and salesy in an attempt to pitch and persuade.

Let's consider how your prospects joined your email list.

They opted in to a free offer.

The free offer is set in place in order to allow your prospects to gain clarity on what you recommend as a strategy to best solve their business challenges.

If subsequent emails are salesy, pitch and persuade, then you're likely going to get a high rate of unsubscriptions from your list.

POWERHOUSE EMAIL

If your list was built on, "Top 5 ways to (solve their challenge)..."

Then you follow up with a campaign like this:

That screams salesy and desperate.

I know there are cases where flash sales do convert, and in some cases you risk your margins to acquire these new clients, but the long-term benefits are minimal.

These customers and clients are leaving after just 3 months, 6 months and some businesses are lucky to keep them around for 12 months.

Those customer and clients were not acquired on a value-centric basis, they're acquired based on a price point, and I am here to tell you, if you acquired a client on price, they're more inclined to leave on price.

POWERHOUSE EMAIL

DO Educate and Engage

How Ian Insurance Wrote 41 Policies in 30 Days with Email

Hey Brian,

One of the biggest challenges with any independent Insurance Agents includes finding qualified prospects.

The WORST way to finding qualified prospects is by purchasing or renting lead lists.

Let's be honest. If the leads were both qualified and eager to buy, nobody would be selling their lists.

Luckily Ian Insurance has shared some of this best practices to writing 41 policies in just 30 days.

Today, we are sharing that interview between Ian Insurance and our staff, and you may be surprised with the simplicity of his strategy that cost him just $100.

[Click to Read the Interview]

In this example of an email intended to educate and engage, we may target our list of Independent Insurance Agents who are looking for more information on leveraging low-cost and guerrilla marketing strategies to lead generation.

If the other email was sent to their inbox, they may unsubscribe.

If this email is present, you're looking at a strong click-through rate, and potentially the purchase of a low-level offer which includes Ian Insurance's strategy and your product, service or solution.

POWERHOUSE EMAIL

POWERHOUSE EMAIL

OTHER BOOKS FROM THE AUTHOR

If you enjoyed this book, consider looking at other books from Curtis DeCora.

Potent Prospecting:

The Practical Guide to Real-World Strategies for Filling Empty Pipelines

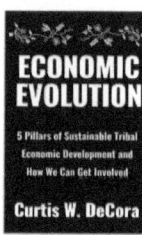

Economic Evolution:

5 Pillars to Sustainable Tribal Economic Development

Powerhouse Calling:

How to leverage phone prospecting to fill your sales pipeline with qualified prospects

Ultimate Sales Prospecting Playbook

The ultimate guide to prospecting and filling sales pipelines for high earners

POWERHOUSE EMAIL

POWERHOUSE EMAIL

THANK YOU

I want to thank you for taking the time to read Powerhouse Email, and learn more about the power of a structured and permission-based sales solution via email.

For more information, resources, tools, and blog posts, go to: www.PotentProspecting.us to learn more about prospecting strategies, techniques, tips and methods for filling your sales pipeline with more qualified prospects.

From the team at Superior Marketing, and my children, Kendal and Adel, we thank you for supporting our initiatives and efforts to bring quality content to the masses of sales professionals.

Best wishes!

Curtis DeCora | Principal
Superior Marketing
PO Box 794
Hayward WI 54843
www.HaywardMarketing.us

www.ingramcontent.com/pod-product-compliance
Lightning Source LLC
Chambersburg PA
CBHW020547220526
45463CB00006B/2222